This book has been donated
by Northland Press and Justin Industries, Inc.
For a complete catalog of Northland Press books, write:
Northland Press, P.O. Box N, Flagstaff, Arizona 86002

FROM
ICE MOUNTAIN

FROM ICE MOUNTAIN

Indian Settlement of the Americas

By DON PERCEVAL

with an Introduction by Frank Waters

NORTHLAND PRESS   FLAGSTAFF, ARIZONA

INTRODUCTION

IT IS A GREAT PRIVILEGE to add a few introductory comments to this book written and illustrated by the late Don Perceval. In a way, it belatedly returns the compliment he paid me fourteen years ago when he illustrated a limited edition of my novel, *The Man Who Killed the Deer*, that was published by Northland Press.

Don Perceval's stature as an acute observer and painter of the Southwest was achieved by three decades of work and study. When only nineteen years old, his familiarity with the Hopi Indians enabled him to illustrate Harry C. James's *Treasure of the Hopitu*. Continuing his painting of the Hopis, he was made a member of the tribe in 1951.

His high-water *Navajo Sketch Book* of line drawings, sketches, and watercolors of the "Deneh" and their immense wilderness reservation, the largest in the United States, was first published in 1962 and has been twice reprinted. Three years later he depicted the Pueblo Indians of Taos, New Mexico, for my book, and ten years after that, in 1975, Natachee Scott Momaday's *Owl in the Cedar Tree* appeared containing more than fifty of his illustrations again depicting Navajo life.

One other work I must mention is his large painting of the infamous fight of October 26, 1881, in Tombstone, Arizona, misnamed since then as the fight at the O.K. Corral. Commissioned by John D. Gilchriese, this painting reflects Perceval's meticulous regard for historical accuracy.

Nor was he less mindful of the events and customs of the early Spanish period. Perhaps no other artist possessed such a comprehensive knowledge of the details of the *conquistadores'* dress and accoutrements and the developing styles of their horses' bridles, saddles, and stirrups. And he knew the cattle brands of the later Anglo ranchers.

Hesitant as I am to assume the mantle of a critic, I believe that his approach to art shows two working techniques. His lively sketches and drawings in the *Navajo Sketch Book* are achieved by their sure, dramatic lines. In contrast, his illustrations for *The Man Who Killed the Deer* appeal by their solid, monochromatic forms. What wonderfully evocative illustrations they are! No sharp lines delineating the figures. Just the soft shapes of man, deer, bird, and star bearing the color blue — the blue of Taos pueblo's sacred Blue Lake.

In *From Ice Mountain* the deceptively simple figures combine the appeal of line, form, and color, the lines revealing details of periodic change. These illustrations depict the early appearance of Indians in America, the arrival of their Spanish conquerors and the conflict between them, and the Indian ceremonials that still continue today. What a preposterous span of history to accomplish in just sixty-six pages!

Mr. Perceval achieves it, I believe, by his sense of history as a flowing stream of constant change. And this is our reaction as we turn the pages, watching history unfold. His intuition is sound. Perpetual movement generating life and change was a philosophic concept of the ancient Mayas and Aztecs. The Aztec symbol for Movement, *Ollin*, was embodied as the 17th day sign or hieroglyph in the esoteric sacred calendar of Mesoamerica.

The success of painting does not rest on photographic representation of the subject. It lies in selecting those significant details which bring into focus the inner life of the subject, be it a portrait, a still life, or a landscape. And this is achieved by the increment — the saving grace — of art, which reveals those special qualities not apparent to the outer eye. These Indians moving through the dim prehistoric past were imaginatively conceived from long study and recreated with high art. This is what makes them come alive.

I didn't know Don Perceval intimately. He lived in Santa Barbara, California, and I in Taos, New Mexico; but we met often in Tucson, Arizona, where he went periodically to pursue his researches. He had many cronies to visit there. They included John Gilchriese, then field historian for the University of Arizona; Art Woodward, former curator of history and anthropology at the Los Angeles County Museum; and Charles di Peso, director of the Amerind Foundation, who was excavating the prehistoric ruins of Casas Grandes in Chihuahua, and with whom Perceval worked for a time. What rousing meetings, what noisy arguments, these historians had!

I became better acquainted with Perceval when he came to stay with me in Taos for several days. He had brought with him a series of color sketches portraying the evolving changes in Indian dress, and we hoped it might be possible to collaborate on a text to accompany them. Fortunately nothing came for our prolonged discussion: his present brief remarks on each group of figures reveal better than a wordy narrative the meaning of the finished paintings.

And now a note about the artist himself. Born in England in 1908, and proud of his British ancestry, he was always a gentleman

vii

in thought and manner — a far cry from the homespun southwesterner brought up in cowboy boots and Levi's. Early in his life, his family moved from England to Southern California where Perceval attended Hollywood High School and studied at the Chouinard Art Institute in Los Angeles. To complete his studies he returned to London and entered the Heatherly School of Art and the Royal College of Art. Then it was back to America, where he continued to grow more familiar with the land, the people, and the history of the Southwest — those subjects to which he could apply his talent and training.

World War II interrupted his work. He returned again to England and served for six years in the British Royal Navy. After his tour of duty ended, he came back to his adopted homeland, where he succumbed once more to his fascination with the memorabilia of his special field: Indians, conquistadores, outlaws, six-guns, bridles, and cattle brands. Not romantically, as most lesser artists might, but realistically, with an interest founded on his sound British and American art studies, and his continuing research into historical traditions.

Living in his large, gracious home in Santa Barbara, endowed with a private income which enabled him to paint and travel throughout the Southwest, Mr. Perceval was not obliged to turn out a large volume of commercial paintings to suit popular taste. He painted what and as he pleased. If I, for one, wish he had produced more, the quality of what he achieved is very high.

It is sad that he died a few months before publication of this book. Yet he will be remembered as an acknowledged authority on the Southwest he loved so much, and a significant translator of its ways of life. To this, his book bears witness.

FRANK WATERS

viii

FROM
ICE MOUNTAIN

Three Asian hunters moved quietly along the right flank of a herd of reindeer. They were of the Right Flank People, as had been their forefathers, and to hunt elsewhere would be to offend either the Left Flank People or the Following Behind People. This could lead to fighting.

Each year the Right Flank People followed the seasonal movements of the herd: northward as the spring came and the snow withdrew, westward along the southern ramparts of the great ice mountains, and southward again as the weather grew severe and the winter storms blew in from the Arctic.

There came a year when the herds were restless and seemed unwilling to start their northward movement. The mild west wind had broken the grip of winter, and the thaw had filled every stream bed with rushing water. The first wild flowers budded and bloomed, and still the reindeer grazed in aimless circles.

The worried hunters gathered around the old men to see if, in their wisdom, they could find a way to appease the offended spirits of the animals they had killed. Not even the oldest man could remember a year such as this. The headmen spoke mysteriously of sacrifice.

As the whole band silently watched the herd, a large male with enormous spreading antlers raised his head and sniffed the breeze. He walked a few stiff-legged paces to the east before lowering his head and relaxing his muscles. The whole herd stopped grazing and followed him.

The Asian hunters quickly gathered their few belongings, and all that day, and for many days, they followed the long line of migrating reindeer across the rolling tundra and into the unknown east. Rocky hills appeared before them only to be left behind as the daily march continued.

On a day many thousands of years ago, the reindeer herd and its satellite bands of hunters came out of the broken hills and down to an ancient shoreline. Although waves had once broken on this rocky shore, the level of the sea had been lowered, and the reindeer set out over miles of exposed ocean floor toward other hills, blue

in the distance. The hunters followed them down into this great
valley and splashed through a mile or two of shallow seawater.
Gradually they climbed toward the hills that had once been islands
and that would be islands again. Although the hunters never knew
it, they had left Asia and come to America.

These were not the first hunters to leave their native Asia and to journey to America. Nor were they the last of the many bands and tribes that would follow either herds or their wandering instincts toward new hunting grounds. All drifted slowly southward to the more moderate climate of the great forests.

Each year for hundreds of years the descendants of these hunters spread over the varied face of the American continent. And each year for thousands of years they adapted themselves to their new environment, changing their customs and their clothing, abandoning the heavy arctic clothing of their ancestors.

Small groups of these very ancient Indians followed the game trails onto the forested plateaus of the Southwest. Here great elephants struck fear into their hearts by their trumpeting and wolves snarled and fought over their kills, but the hunters stayed awhile.

12

As they moved southward, the tracks they left soon disappeared in the waving grasslands. They left behind the charcoal of their burned-out campfires, the bones from their meals of camel or prehistoric horsemeat, and a few finely made spear points of stone, for us to marvel at.

Their way was into the jungles of Mexico and Central America where they delighted in wearing the bright-colored plumage of the tropical birds. Developing new ways, finding new foods, they met other bands of Indians that had come before them or by a different route.

As they hunted and explored, moving toward South America, they mingled with, fought with, absorbed or were absorbed by these other bands. Only vague legends reminded them of their original land. Finally, at the southmost tip of the southern continent, the vanguard of this human tide could go no farther.

Group after group, band after band, had fanned out along the many trails of this southward migration. Each followed its destiny into steaming tropical jungles and river bottoms, or climbed to find homes in the rarefied atmosphere of the highest mountain ranges.

Some found the more arid country to their liking while others disappeared into the rolling grasslands of both continents. Each group slowly took on an identity with new ways of living in widely differing environments. New words for new things came into common use. Clothing varied according to climate and innovations became tribal marks.

The wandering hunters came to pleasant valleys and stayed. Their numbers increased, their crude shelters became permanent houses, and they gathered fruits and seeds from the surrounding countryside. Hunters became hunter-farmers as they learned to live from crops of their own planting.

It was here, somewhere in the highlands of the valley of Mexico, that through endless plantings of some unknown seed, the first small ears of corn came into being. Selecting the best seed from each harvest for planting produced larger and larger ears until farming replaced hunting as the principal source of food.

Slowly, the knowledge of corn growing spread both north and south, following the dim trade trails which covered primitive America. Agriculture and permanent villages became the foundation for the ex-hunters' first steps toward the high state of civilization finally achieved in the Americas.

The ancestors of the Mayas planted little fields of corn long before they became the mighty rulers of Yucatán and Guatemala. They had lived alongside their plantings for centuries before the first stones were laid in the building of the great temples at Tikal, Labna, and Chichén Itzá.

21

Year after year the cornfields of Central America produced their golden harvests. And year after year the corn seed was traded to other groups of hunters who, in their turn, learned to wield planting sticks instead of hunting spears. But fifteen hundred miles to the northwest lived those who had wearied of marching south.

They had stayed and watched in fear as the great forests were swept away and enormous salt water lakes covered the valleys where they once had hunted mammoths and horses. Flatland burst upward as mountain ranges were born and volcanos showered the earth with cinders and ash.

There were those who stopped along the way of the southward migration to settle where the climate was mild. The minimum of clothing and the crudest of shelters served them adequately.

The low desert country supplied them with enough cactus fruit, seeds, lizards, and lesser animals to fill their stomachs with little effort.

Toward the end of the first century A.D., groups of men from the northern perimeter of the corn-growing culture of Central America set out northward in search of new planting grounds. The wind soon erased the imprints of their sandaled feet, and the desert of Sonora kept no record of their passing.

The primitive desert Indians saw them coming and spied upon them as the newcomers examined the soil of the river bottoms and set up housekeeping in sheltered caves nearby. They watched with fascination as these Cave Dwellers cleared and planted their little cornfields; with them, corn had reached the Southwest.

Drawn out of the south by half understood legends of an ancestral homeland to the north, others of the corn-planting peoples of Central America straggled across the Rio Grande. They left some of their number to live awhile in the canyons of Texas and traveled still farther until they wandered into the labyrinthine can-

yons north of the San Juan. Here the sun-drenched rock overhangs, innocent of human occupancy, offered shelter to people destined to become Cliff Dwellers and Basketmakers at a time soon after the year A.D. 200.

Other Basketmakers came into the Southwest by a more westerly route. They followed the Colorado River into Utah or the Gila and the Verde into northern Arizona. They too perched their homes like swallows' nests high in the cliff faces and planted their cornfields in the well-watered canyons below.

Theirs was a different corn than that of the Cave Dwellers indicating that, even before they had taken the long trail to the north, the original Central American corn had sported into several distinct varieties. During the centuries pottery-making was discovered and constantly improving houses looked more and more like

the forerunners of the Great Pueblos. For hundreds of years the peaceful life of the Southwest involved each generation of early Puebloans tending their cornfields, herding their flocks of domestic turkeys, and decorating their pottery with increasingly beautiful designs. Now they lived in the center of a widening web of trade

trails over which adventurous Indian traders carried their wares. They brought seashells from the far Pacific and the farther Gulf of Mexico. They brought turquoise from distant desert mines, red ochre, and obsidian; all these were worn by the beautiful Pueblo women as they welcomed home their farmer husbands.

By the year A.D. 900 the first of the Great Pueblos was being built. During the next three hundred years the life of the Pueblo peoples reached the height of its primitive affluence and culture. From the large trading town of Casas Grandes in Chihuahua representatives of a Central Mexican culture furnished the macaw and

parrot feathers so desired by the Puebloans. The great kivas of every village erupted long lines of beautifully costumed dancers as the Kachinas kept the Puebloans and their world in perfect balance. It was fitting that the dancers should wear the bright feathers from a land deep in their legendary past.

Once more the urge to move swept the Pueblo people of the Southwest. Long before the great drought began in A.D. 1276, village after village emptied as the population drifted away southward. It could have been that the overworked cornfields no longer produced corn as nourishing as it had been. It could have been that the mesa tops had been stripped of cedar and pinon, and without firewood, cooking simple meals was impossible.

To the east and south of the Great Pueblos lay the middle reaches of the Rio Grande and the surrounding land, unused except by wandering hunters. While evidence is lacking, it may be that the villages begun along the Rio Grande at this time were built by those who had left the Pueblos of the San Juan–Mesa Verde area.

The wild Chichimec came southward into the valley of Mexico and took over the lands of the Otomi. Adopting the Otomi culture, mastering it, and improving upon it, they were so proud of themselves that they called themselves Toltec — the civilized people. The Toltec expanded the trade trails which ran up the west coast of Mexico. They established a trading center at Casas Grandes from which lesser trails led to the Puebloan villages in the valley of the Chaco. For more than two hundred years the Toltec traders passed north and south with their trade goods until they were overthrown by other wild Chichimecans — the Aztec.

Of the great Athabascan tribes — the Chipweyans, the Yellow Knives, the Dog Ribs, the Sekani, Navajo, and Apache — only the Navajo and Apache continued their southward migration.

The Navajo called themselves "Deneh," meaning The People. Nomads and raiders, they arrived in the Southwest a comparatively short time before the Spaniards landed in Mexico.

The wild Deneh often materialized out of the very edges of
the corn plantings so silently that the twang of a bow string and
the thunk of an arrow hitting its mark were often all the warning
the Pueblo farmers had. The little cornfields became places of fear
as the blood of more and more peaceful Tewas, Keres, and Zuñis

sank into the sand among the corn stalks. The great kiva drums throbbed out messages of alarm as the young men painted the warrior marks upon their cheeks and fashioned bows and spears with which to defend their ancient villages.

Toltec authority was gone. The Aztecs were too busy with unrest in Central Mexico to police the trade trails. Aware of this, the wild Indians waited to plunder the few trading parties brave enough to attempt the route.

In time Aztec traders took over the northern trade. But the

Great Pueblos stood empty, and the subject people of Casas Grandes were declining. Aztec trade and authority in the north gradually diminished and then ceased; the wild Opatas from the surrounding hills attacked ailing Casas Grandes which died in an orgy of blood and smoke.

New trade trails deep into Mexico were over one hundred and fifty years old when, along with the latest consignment of macaw feathers, came startling news of an alien landing. Light-colored men and a number of strange animals had come in from the sea and were marching steadily toward the valley of Mexico.

At first these travelers were treated with respect and offered the hospitality due to all travelers. But the Spaniards became arrogant and overbearing in their demands for gold, and the welcome hardened into hostility. When opposed, the invaders left great swaths of dead and dying Indians as evidence of their invincibility.

45

The dreadful news was relayed to Tenochtitlán, the hub of the Aztec empire. The soldier societies of Montezuma's army closed their ranks and waited, but the Emperor chose another way and relied upon diplomacy, sending his ambassadors to reason with the Spaniards.

Courtly negotiations did not slow the march through Mexico although they made it easier for the intruders to reach the outskirts of the capitol without a major battle. Once there the Spaniards could see no further need for diplomacy when the gold they sought was on every side.

Frustrated by delay, the Spanish struck. The conquistadors lived by the sword and were not noted for either their humanitarianism or their diplomacy; Toledo steel could quickly decide any argument. Their undoubted courage was met by courage in equal measure as the Aztec warriors overcame their fear of the horses and hurled themselves against the lines of charging horsemen. For

days the outcome remained in doubt. The Aztecs threw back the invaders and seemed capable of driving them to the sea so great was their fighting strength. But feathered shields and stone-edged wooden swords proved to be no match for European armor and the bloodied blades of Toledo.

Once more the Spaniards entered the fabulous city of Tenochtitlán. Street by street and house by house they hacked their way toward the palace of the Emperor Montezuma. Bright-feathered fighting men lay in broken heaps in every alley before this work of butchery ended, and the Aztec empire was crushed forever.

Never again would the vast continents of the Americas be free of their European conquerors. Never would the native Americans continue their spectacular rise — from wandering hunters to builders of great cities and makers of exquisite art. The heights they might have reached lay with their bodies in the dust.

51

Life in the Southwest continued as an uneasy balance. The Navajo and Apache continued to raid outlying cornfields but the Pueblo warriors made them pay in blood for any attempt to penetrate the villages — except when they came by twos and threes to trade. Although the people of the Southwest had heard of the conquest of Mexico, it had affected them not at all. And the news

of a few white men wandering up the Rio Grande before turning south into Mexico had made them feel that earlier stories of Spanish power must be exaggerated. But with Núñez Cabeza de Vaca and the staggering survivors of the Narváez expedition was the giant Estévan.

No matter how the wild stories of the Seven Golden Cities of Cíbola began after Cabeza de Vaca led his party back to Mexico, the Moor Estévan was quick to take advantage of them. Returning northward, supposedly to scout a route for an expedition which would follow, Estévan gathered an admiring train of Opatas and

southern Pimas as he swaggered along dressed in a strange mixture of European garments and native feathers and turquoise. The wooden crosses he was told to leave as guideposts for Fray Marcos de Niza, following a day's journey behind, soon turned into feather-decorated standards as he neared Háwikuh and his own violent end.

Marcos de Niza never entered the Zuñi city of Háwikuh or any other of the villages of the Southwest. Perhaps he saw them in the distance when their rock and adobe walls glowed golden in the rays of the setting sun. The tales of golden cities were enough to spur on the gold-hungry Spaniards who were riding northward

under Francisco Vásquez de Coronado. Up through the sandy wastes of Sonora and the cactus-studded desert of southern Arizona, they rode in sweating discomfort. Before they reached the pine forests of the Mogollon, reports of their progress were relayed to Háwikuh. Because of tales from Mexico, no welcome awaited them there.

A shower of arrows was their greeting from the Zuñis. As they withdrew to reconsider, the Spaniards must have remembered the valiant fighting men of Tenochtitlán, Tlaxcala, and Culiacán, and to have realized that this city would not fall to them easily. They advanced steadily with drawn swords and ready arquebuses through a further hail of arrows and stones hurled from the roof

tops. They chopped their way from plaza to plaza and conquered only when those same roof tops and all the doorways were littered with corpses. By nightfall Háwikuh had received a mortal blow. Only then did the Spaniards stop to consider that they had seen not one ounce of gold.

As Pedro de Tovar and his soldiers climbed over the rim of the eastmost mesa of Tusayán, they were met by the Hopis with a baffling combination of quiet hostility and mystic fatalism. Although the Spanish *entrada* had changed forever the ancient life of the Southwest, in some ways the intruders were influenced more strongly than the original residents. For four hundred years

endless waves of alien explorers, trappers, traders, missionaries, and tourists have come and have fallen under the strange spell of the Indian country. Yet the efforts of these people to prod more than a small number of the southwestern Indians into conforming to the twentieth century have been a failure.

They came from the cities where they worked: from Winslow and Flagstaff, from Phoenix and Los Angeles. They drove up the new paved road to the top of the mesa and parked their cars and pickups in front of their family homes. They had come to see the

Kachinas who were dancing the Home Dance before going to their homes on the high mountain peaks. Only after the quiet and rest of fall would they come again to bring new life to another year.

In the morning the people watched; those who purified the path of the dancers with cornmeal came from the mesa edge. Each of them wore only a kilt and one small downy feather in his long hair and carried a sack of sacred cornmeal to sprinkle on the dancers

— to "feed" the Kachinas. Forming a double line, the Kachinas danced. The lines rotated slowly in opposite directions, turning and turning yet again. They danced this final dance in a stately and reverent manner.

DESIGNED BY MARK SANDERS
AND MICHAEL HOLLAR
COMPOSED IN LINOTYPE ALDUS
WITH DISPLAY LINES
IN HANDSET PALATINO
PRINTED ON WARREN'S OLDE STYLE
AT THE PRESS IN THE PINES

NORTHLAND PRESS

BOUND BY ROSWELL BOOKBINDING
PHOENIX